THE
WACO
STANDOFF

THE
WACO
STANDOFF

BY SCOTT GILLAM

CONTENT CONSULTANT
EUGENE V. GALLAGHER
ROSEMARY PARK PROFESSOR,
DEPARTMENT OF RELIGIOUS STUDIES
CONNECTICUT COLLEGE

ABDO
Publishing Company

CREDITS

Published by ABDO Publishing Company, PO Box 398166, Minneapolis, MN 55439. Copyright © 2014 by Abdo Consulting Group, Inc. International copyrights reserved in all countries. No part of this book may be reproduced in any form without written permission from the publisher. The Essential Library™ is a trademark and logo of ABDO Publishing Company.

Printed in the United States of America,
North Mankato, Minnesota
102013
012014

 THIS BOOK CONTAINS AT LEAST 10% RECYCLED MATERIALS.

Editor: Melissa York
Series Designer: Becky Daum

Photo credits: Susan Weems/AP Images, cover, 2; Waco Tribune Herald/AP Images, 6; AP Images, 13, 22, 24, 89; Barry Thumma/AP Images, 16; Isaiah Shook/Shutterstock Images, 18; Angela K. Brown/AP Images, 28; Bob E. Daemmrich/Sygma/Corbis, 34; Rex USA, 38; Red Line Editorial, 43, 48; Rick Bowmer/AP Images, 44, 46; Derek Lloyd Lovelock, right, and Renos Avraam/AP Images, 52; George Widman/AP Images, 56; David Phillip/AP Images, 63, 71; Everett Collection, 66; Pat Sullivan/AP Images, 74; Ron Heflin/AP Images, 78, 86; G. Reed Schumann/Reuters/Corbis, 80; Charles Bennett/AP Images, 82; Rod Aydelotte/Waco Herald Tribune/AP Images, 84; Bill Janscha/AP Images, 93

Library of Congress Control Number: 2013946966

Cataloging-in-Publication Data

Gillam, Scott.
The Waco standoff / Scott Gillam.
    p. cm. -- (Essential events)
Includes bibliographical references and index.
ISBN 978-1-62403-261-5
1. Waco Branch Davidian Disaster, Tex., 1993--Juvenile literature. 2. Koresh, David, 1959-1993--Juvenile literature. 3. Branch Davidians--Juvenile literature.   I. Title.
976.4--dc23

                                                            2013946966

CONTENTS

CHAPTER
ONE

TO ACT OR
TO WAIT?

It was April 1993. Members of the Branch Davidians religious group had been confined in the Mount Carmel Center—their home near Waco, Texas—for almost 50 days. Hundreds of armed local, state, and federal law enforcement officials surrounded the center. The officials had tried unsuccessfully to serve the group with warrants to search for illegal weapons. The officials also wanted to arrest the group's leader, David Koresh. Koresh was suspected of manufacturing or possessing illegal weapons. But Koresh and most of his followers would not come out, and law enforcement would not back down.

Although they did not know it, law officials and the Branch Davidians were approaching the climax of the standoff. The chain of events had begun on February 28, 1993. The Bureau of Alcohol, Tobacco, and Firearms (ATF) had launched an armed raid on the Mount

David Koresh and his followers practiced a religion few outsiders agreed with or understood.

Carmel compound. In the initial confrontation, six Branch Davidians were killed and an unknown number wounded, including Koresh.[1] It is calculated there were approximately 124 people in the compound when the shooting started.[2] Sixteen ATF agents were wounded and four killed.[3] No one agrees who shot first, and each side blames the other. After the firefight ended, an uneasy cease-fire continued for weeks.

Koresh was a 34-year-old high school dropout. He had the ability to memorize vast portions of the Bible and argue from scripture. With these skills, he was able to convince his followers he was the Messiah. In the book of Revelation, the last book in the Bible, the Messiah will lead his followers to the millennial kingdom after the final battle between good and evil. To his critics, however, Koresh seemed deluded and possibly suicidal. These critics believed Koresh wanted to completely control the physical and mental lives of his followers. Outside observers worried Koresh might encourage his followers to commit mass suicide, believing the siege was a sign of the end of the world.

Different Frames of Reference

Koresh's followers and law enforcement were at a standoff. Each side saw the issues quite differently. For most law enforcement officials, the case was simple. There was evidence the Branch Davidians had broken laws about firearms. The officials' job was to enforce those laws. These officials had been watching the Mount Carmel Center for months. ATF agent Robert Rodriguez had infiltrated the group, and members had shown him some of their weapons.

WAS KORESH SUICIDAL?

During the crisis, the FBI consulted with several psychoanalysts. The FBI wanted to know whether Koresh was likely to be suicidal and whether he would plan a mass suicide for his followers. The authorities worried about a mass suicide because of the previous actions of a US religious group, the Peoples Temple. Nine hundred members of the group who were living in Jonestown, Guyana, had committed suicide together in 1978.[4] The Jonestown mass suicide loomed large in everyone's memories, and the FBI did not want a repeat at Waco.

The psychoanalysts disagreed whether Koresh was likely to encourage a group suicide. So did some former group members and group members who exited the compound during the standoff. Five group members who came out during the standoff said they were unaware of any mass suicide plans. Others said there were suicide plans. In the absence of any consensus, the FBI itself made no decision one way or the other on this issue.

For the Branch Davidians, on the other hand, the issue was the group's right to practice its religion, own legal firearms, and be protected from unreasonable searches and seizures. These rights are guaranteed under the First, Second, and Fourth Amendments to the US Constitution. During the 51-day siege, group member Wayne Martin, a Harvard-trained lawyer, and Koresh's attorney, Dick DeGuerin, would make these points to anyone who would listen.

Janet Reno, Children's Advocate

The new US attorney general, Janet Reno, was the one person most responsible for deciding how best to resolve the standoff. Reno took office on March 12, after the standoff had been in progress for almost two weeks.

Throughout her previous career, Reno had developed a strong reputation both as a prosecutor of criminals and a defender of children. She had been elected four times as a county attorney in her native Florida. Reno was both praised and criticized for her aggressive pursuit of convictions in several child abuse cases during this period. When children's well-being and lives were at risk, Reno's instinct was to protect children at all costs. She believed in negotiation and other nonviolent means as the best way to resolve differences.

Early negotiations between law enforcement and the Branch Davidians had been successful. By mid-March, the Branch Davidians had sent out half of the 42 children inside the center, along with a few adults.[6] As the siege went into its third week, however, law enforcement officials seemed headed toward a deadlock. The two sides seemed to have less and less room to compromise. The Davidians just wanted to be left alone. The FBI wanted them to surrender, with some facing arrest. Negotiators pleaded for mothers to come out with their children. Negotiators sent in tapes, letters, and articles that were sympathetic to Koresh's religious concerns. These gestures sometimes produced meetings between the Branch Davidians and negotiators that seemed to cool down tempers. Other government actions, such as playing loud music and other noises at night to upset the Davidians' sleep, caused tempers to flare up again. The nerves of group members and law enforcement were becoming more frazzled. This general jumpiness seemed more and more likely to cause a confrontation that could lead to a tragic end.

More than 80 group members remained inside the Mount Carmel Center by the end of March.[7] In addition, 720 law enforcement officials were on the scene.[8] Several hundred members of the press had also gathered in nearby Waco to cover the event. The publicity generated by restless reporters hungry for a story also added to the mounting pressure felt by law enforcement officials.

Considering Tear Gas

It seemed unlikely to most of the FBI agents that large numbers of the remaining group members would come out willingly. Beginning on March 22, the negotiators considered a new plan. Tear gas could be gradually introduced into the center. Tear gas was considered a nonlethal alternative to firearms. It would cause crying and choking that would hopefully force those inside to

The Branch Davidians lived in a large compound in Waco, Texas.

leave the immediate area. The gas would gradually be injected into the center, building by building, over a two-day period. This method would theoretically give group members plenty of time to exit.

After the details were worked out, law enforcement officials presented the plan to Attorney General Reno in

Washington, DC, on April 12. Reno was suspicious of the plan at first. "Why now, why not wait?" she asked.[9] She demanded proof the gas would not cause chronic harm to pregnant women and young children. A medical expert told Reno there had been no studies of the effects of tear gas on children, but "anecdotal evidence was convincing that there would be no permanent injury."[10] Would Reno accept this argument, even though it was not scientifically proven?

The group members had enough food for at least a year. Reno wondered, however, if the water supply could be cut off. She was told Koresh was rationing the water supply, and the group had enough to last a long time. FBI bullets could easily puncture the group's water tank, thereby draining their water supply. But since the early cease-fire, the FBI agents had kept their promise not to fire on the center unless they themselves were fired upon.

Reno met several times with government officials. She still seemed unconvinced the tear gas option would work. Officials again assured her the tear gas was nonlethal. They said it would not cause permanent harm to children. They strongly believed it would not catch fire, even though manufacturers had issued warnings to the contrary. Several experts believed Koresh's behavior did not show him to be suicidal. Thus they believed he would come out with his followers if the tear gas were used. Even so, Reno denied the plan three times. She still believed waiting was safer.

Reno Changes Her Mind

Then FBI director William Sessions spoke to Reno on April 16. For some reason, Reno changed her mind. Later, she explained she believed there was child abuse taking place within the compound. Today, it is unclear whether there was any abuse during the standoff.

Reno no longer expressed disapproval of the tear gas plan. Instead, she asked for a

THE FIRST FEMALE US ATTORNEY GENERAL

President Bill Clinton appointed Janet Reno in 1993. She served until 2001. This was the second-longest tenure of any US attorney general. Reno was the oldest of four children, born in Florida in 1938. She graduated from Cornell University and then attended Harvard Law School. Reno was one of only 16 women in a class of 500.[11] Reno served in various judiciary positions in Florida. Then she became the first female Florida state attorney at the county level. Reno held this position for 15 years before becoming US attorney general. After, she made an unsuccessful run for governor in Florida. In recent years, her activities have been slowed by Parkinson's disease. Yet Reno remains a role model among women for her achievements in politics and in the professional world.

Janet Reno was sworn in as President Bill Clinton's attorney general on March 12, after the standoff in Waco was already in progress.

documented statement to be prepared. The statement would show "the situation inside the compound, the progress of the negotiations, and the merits of the proposal."[12]

The next day, Reno was satisfied all the points in the plan were supported. She noted she had the right to stop the plan at any time. She promised, however, to leave tactical decisions in the hands of law enforcement officers on the scene. Reno approved the tear gas plan and briefed President Bill Clinton on April 18. Time would soon tell whether she had made the right decision.

CHAPTER TWO

A SHORT HISTORY OF THE DAVIDIANS

The word *sect* is often used to describe a religious group whose beliefs, usually centering on a specific doctrine or leader, are regarded as dissenting or extreme compared to the related, more mainstream religion. In popular usage, the word *cult* may also be used to describe a system of religious beliefs and practices, but these beliefs are usually regarded as unorthodox or false. While widely viewed as a cult by the media, the public, and most government officials, the Branch Davidians had their roots in the beliefs of Seventh-day Adventists, a major Christian group whose beliefs emphasize the imminent end of the world and the Second Coming of Christ.

The First Seventh-day Adventists

Inspired by the teachings of William Miller, the Seventh-day Adventists (SDA) began in the 1840s.

The Branch Davidians' interpretation of the book of Revelation led many outsiders to perceive them as a cult.

THE DAVIDIANS AND THE SEVENTH-DAY ADVENTISTS

Despite having split from the SDA, the general characteristics and beliefs of the Davidians and the SDA remained fairly similar. Both groups focused on the "end times" described in the book of Revelation. Both celebrated the Sabbath on Saturday, observed similar dietary restrictions, and had what journalist Dick Reavis described as "an aloofness from, and distrust of, government."[2]

By the 2010s, they had become an international group with more than 17 million members.[1]

In 1934, Victor Houteff, a member of the SDA, accused the Adventists of neglecting their primary mission of preparing members for the end of the world through scriptural study. Houteff was barred from the church for making these accusations. He and a small group of followers moved from California to Texas in 1935. They settled on land near Waco. Houteff later named his new group the Davidian Seventh-day Adventists.

Under Houteff's skilled leadership, the group grew. At one time, the group even maintained its own school and college. Most of the Davidian Bible study focused on the Old Testament prophets and the writings of the early Christians, especially the book of Revelation. Similar to followers of Judaism, the Davidians recognized Passover and some other Jewish holidays. They marked Saturday as their day of rest, and they did not eat pork. The flag that flew over the Mount Carmel Center featured a Star of David, a symbol associated with Judaism. After Houteff's death in 1955, Houteff's wife, Florence, briefly led the group, but follower Ben Roden soon assumed leadership. Roden's nickname "the Branch" would later become part of the group's name.

David Koresh: Victim and Survivor

Born on August 17, 1959, David Koresh was the first child of a 14-year-old single mother, Bonnie Clark, and a 20-year-old father whom Koresh never met.

VICTOR HOUTEFF, FOUNDER OF THE DAVIDIANS

Born in 1885, Victor Houteff was a Bulgarian immigrant to the United States. Ejected from the SDA, he and his dozen followers moved to Waco in 1935. According to Malachi 4:5 in the Bible, the prophet Elijah will appear before the Second Coming of Christ. Many of Houteff's followers believed Houteff himself was the same Elijah reborn, sent by God to prepare his followers for the end times. Houteff mailed his teachings to 100,000 members of the SDA throughout the United States.[3] Thus he spread the name of the Davidians, eventually attracting hundreds of members.

Lonely and physically abused by relatives as a child, he found refuge in the teachings of his mother's local SDA church. From a young age, he believed he heard God speaking to him. Koresh liked the church's emphasis on

From an early age, Koresh was drawn to teachings about the end of the world.

the Second Coming of Christ, the end of the world (or "end times"), and the reign of the righteous in heaven. He became concerned the SDA church had no current prophet for members to look up to anymore. When Koresh was in his early twenties, he informed his local pastor God wanted Koresh and the pastor's daughter to be husband and wife. The pastor promptly threw him out of the church.

In 1981, Koresh found his way to Mount Carmel, where he was hired as a repairman. By this time, the leader at the compound was 67-year-old Lois Roden, wife of the deceased Ben. Ben had renamed the group the Living Waters Branch, soon also known as the Branch or the Branch Davidians. Roden was looking for a successor to lead the Mount Carmel congregation. Her son George wanted to succeed his mother, but Lois had her doubts. The conflict between mother and son eventually caused as many as half of the members to leave. Lois had won a court case that prevented her son from setting foot on Mount Carmel, but now her energies were at low

VERNON HOWELL, ALSO KNOWN AS DAVID KORESH

David Koresh was born Vernon Wayne Howell. He changed his name to David Koresh in 1990 for what he said were "professional reasons," citing his occupation as "entertainer."[4] Koresh and several other Branch Davidians played in a rock band called Messiah. Both names had deep meaning for Koresh. In the Bible, God promised David one of his descendants would one day rule in heaven. Koresh is the Hebrew version of Cyrus; Cyrus is mentioned in the Bible in Isaiah 45:1 as God's chosen one who conquered Babylon.

Koresh with his wife Rachel and son Cyrus

ebb. In Koresh, Lois found an energetic ally with some political savvy.

By 1984, Koresh had married 14-year-old Rachel Jones. Rachel was the daughter of Perry and Mary Bell Jones, who were loyal supporters of Lois Roden and longtime Mount Carmel residents. The marriage was legal in Texas at the time with parental consent. Koresh's position in the group was getting stronger. Their son Cyrus would be born in 1985, and other children would follow. In the coming years, Koresh would have children with many women, most of whom were his married followers or the daughters of his followers. Koresh considered all of these women his wives as well.

George Roden's Failed Bid for Leadership

George Roden would launch one more attempt to lead the group. In 1984, amid rising tension, Koresh and his band of followers left Mount Carmel and resettled in Palestine, Texas, 100 miles (160 km) away. There they survived for a time living in tents and large wooden packing crates. Lois died in 1986 with the group still split. Faced with doubts about his leadership from his dwindling group of loyalists, Roden tried to drum up support by digging up the coffin containing the body of Anna Hughes. Hughes was a group member who had died 20 years before. Roden then challenged Koresh to a contest to see who could raise Hughes from the dead. Instead of taking on the challenge, Koresh reported Roden to the police for grave tampering in 1987. Authorities told Koresh he would have to prove his charge with photographs of the corpse. Koresh returned with seven armed followers to secure his proof. In the gun battle that followed, Roden was injured. Koresh's group was arrested and charged with attempted murder.

A jury found Koresh's group not guilty. Then law officials arrested Roden for violating the court order that had prohibited him from entering the Mount Carmel property. He was sentenced to six months in

KORESH'S RIVAL, GEORGE RODEN

"Poor George," as he was often called by group members, was not a very inspiring leader.[5] He also had serious physical and mental problems. Roden suffered from Tourette's syndrome, which caused his face to contort and spit to come uncontrollably from his mouth. Roden could also be extremely paranoid, sometimes responding to threats by brandishing an Uzi automatic rifle. Following the shoot-out with Koresh in 1987, Roden had reportedly told him, "I'm not going to come back with BB guns."[6] When Koresh and seven followers were tried for attempted murder after the shoot-out, it was largely because of Roden's delusional testimony the defendants were all freed. Roden later left for Odessa, Texas, and in 1989, he killed a man with an ax. He was sent to an institution for criminals with mental illnesses. Curiously, Roden's wife Amo Bishop Roden returned to Mount Carmel in the middle of 1993 after the standoff. Two years later, she was still there, living in a homemade shack and selling Davidian memorabilia. She told reporter Peter Boyer she had been instructed by God to return and keep the "end-time church" alive.[7] She was one of many who claimed she was the leader of the remaining Branch Davidians after Koresh's death.

jail. In a triumphant mood, Koresh and his followers quickly moved back to Mount Carmel, paid off six years of unpaid taxes, and took complete control of the Branch Davidians in spring 1988. Koresh's study of the Bible and especially the book of Revelation reinforced his belief he was the Messiah. His explanation of God's prophecy in the Seven Seals of Revelation—and his assertion he was the only one who could decode them correctly—solidified his group and won him new followers.

CHAPTER
THREE

THE ROLE OF
THE MEDIA

The Branch Davidians had a rugged existence. They lived in a poorly heated dormitory-like building with no indoor bathrooms. Men and women, including married couples, had separate bedrooms. Some group members worked at jobs in the outside community. Others did jobs inside the center's facilities. These facilities included a chapel, cafeteria, gymnasium, tornado shelter, and swimming pool.

Koresh was initially concerned Roden and his followers might return and attack Mount Carmel. Thus, he kept firearms to protect the group. Koresh also discovered buying and selling firearms was a good way to earn income. A few group members traveled to local gun shows for this purpose. Other businesses that helped support the group included a sewing circle that made and sold survival gear.

The Mount Carmel Center included a metal tower like a silo that stored the group's water, as seen in this model, helping the center be self-sufficient.

In May 1992, a delivery driver reported a suspicious package to the local police. The package, addressed to the group, had broken open during the journey. It revealed firearm parts, dummy grenades, and black powder. The local sheriff notified ATF agents. The ATF wanted to investigate the incident, search the Mount Carmel Center, seize any illegal weapons, and arrest Koresh for possessing an illegal weapon.

THE DAVIDIANS' SURVIVAL GEAR BUSINESS

In addition to Koresh's firearms sales at gun shows around Texas, Davidians made money to support their activities in several ways. The group operated a stall at gun shows around Texas. The survival gear they sold included hunting vests, gas masks, and ammunition magazines, as well as surplus military goods. Davidian women who were skilled tailors sewed the hunting vests.

A Public Relations Opportunity

The ATF likely had another motive for pursuing the case. Like any agency of the government, the ATF depended on funding by Congress. Sharon Wheeler was the public information officer of the ATF. She saw a raid on the group as a chance to create valuable publicity for the bureau. Around that time, several high-profile incidents including a confrontation in Ruby Ridge, Idaho, had cast the agency in a poor light. Favorable media coverage could persuade congressional representatives to increase ATF funding. The budget hearings were to take place less than two weeks after February 28, 1993, the date the ATF planned to raid the Mount Carmel Center.

After months of investigation, the department put together an affidavit with the results of its investigation. The affidavit laid out the department's evidence that Koresh's group manufactured and possessed illegal firearms. It also included information about matters outside the ATF's jurisdiction, including accusations of polygamy, child abuse, and statutory rape. The affidavit was used to get a search warrant from a Texas judge.

THE ATF

For most of its history, the ATF was a part of the US Treasury Department. The US Treasury Department has taxed and regulated alcohol since the United States became a country. The Prohibition Unit rose to prominence after the Eighteenth Amendment, which prohibited the manufacture and sale of alcohol, went into effect in 1920. After the end of Prohibition in 1933, most alcohol consumption became legal. Over the next few decades, the unit's duties shrunk, and its functions were combined with firearms and tobacco taxation and regulation. The ATF had few flashy cases during this time compared to its sister agency, the FBI. The FBI investigated high-profile crimes and had a more respected image. The ATF had some concerns it might be combined with another agency and lose its funding and independence. The ATF came under the umbrella of the Department of Justice in 2003.

Even before the department got the search warrant, events were set in motion as the ATF set up spy cameras in a nearby house to film Davidian activities in the month leading up to the raid. The agency also filmed its own planning and training sessions. Special agent Wheeler's job, as she later admitted to Congress, was

WERE THE DAVIDIANS' FIREARMS ILLEGAL?

In preparing for the February 28 raid, the ATF sought to prove the Davidians possessed illegal automatic weapons. Since that time, the evidence has been disputed. In 1993, it was legal to own both semiautomatic and automatic weapons, as long as the owners of the weapons were approved by local authorities and the weapons were registered by paying a tax. At the time of the standoff, more than 250,000 people in the United States owned legal automatic weapons.[1] According to group member David Thibodeau, however, the Davidians were guilty of not paying the proper registration fees for some of the weapons they possessed. Most of the weapons were in disassembled form. The ATF affidavit falsely claimed the spare parts received by the Davidians were actually a kit for turning the weapons into machine guns. The affidavit also did not show the group had any intent to use the parts to convert a semiautomatic weapon into an automatic one. Legally, the affidavit had to show such intent. The affidavit also included unsubstantiated allegations of child abuse and accused the group of having a lab for making methamphetamines on site— neither of which would have been in the ATF's jurisdiction. Nevertheless, a local magistrate approved the affidavit.

"to show the agency in a good light."[2] With that goal in mind, she equipped every ATF agent with a camera. Wheeler also scheduled a news conference to take place after the raid on February 28—presumably to announce its successful results.

To make sure the media showed up at her post-raid news conference, Wheeler called several local TV stations. She also expected local newspaper reporters to attend. The ATF had learned a valuable piece of information the week before the raid. The *Waco Tribune-Herald* was planning to publish a seven-part article about the Davidians called "The Sinful Messiah." The first part was scheduled to run the day before the raid. The article presented a highly simplified, if not biased, view of the group, based in large part on information

CHILD ABUSE INVESTIGATIONS

Back in April 1992, the Texas Department of Protective and Regulatory Services had investigated child abuse claims against the Branch Davidians and Koresh made by former group members. An agent visited the compound and interviewed children, finding no evidence of child abuse. Investigators later speculated whether the children were unable to speak freely because they were in the compound near adult group members. Others argued it was unlikely the children would have spoken freely under any circumstances. There is evidence Koresh harshly disciplined children and that he had sexual relations with teenage girls, but there is no true consensus on events in the compound before and during the standoff.

The press was on hand to document the ATF raid on the Mount Carmel Center and remained for the rest of the standoff.

from disgruntled people who had left it, including Marc Breault, a former Koresh associate who had been speaking against the leader since 1990. Koresh was described in the lead sentence as someone who "claims a ninth-grade education, married his legal wife when she was 14, enjoys a beer now and then, plays a mean guitar, reportedly packs a 9mm Glock [handgun] . . . and willingly admits he is a sinner without equal."[3] Each fact in the lead sentence was individually true. The sentence as a whole, however, and the series in its entirety, lacked a full perspective. That perspective would have included the religious background, views, and lifestyles of current members as well as the views of its admittedly extreme leader and defectors like Breault.

Making the Davidians Look Bad

Breault had left the Davidians in 1989. He had previously defended Koresh's polygamist practices. Then Koresh pursued Breault's own wife. Breault was also concerned Koresh was having relationships with girls who were too young. Koresh's action led Marc and Elizabeth Breault to leave the Davidians.

Breault then began a media campaign to discredit Koresh in Australia, the home country of several of the group members. His campaign yielded several successes. First, Martin King, Breault's collaborator, got permission in January 1992 to interview Koresh and several group members for the Australian television program *A Current Affair*. The program cast Koresh and the group in a bad light. One example from the program is the following dialogue between Koresh and King:

OPERATION NAME

Top ATF officials named the raid Operation Trojan Horse. This was a reference to the ancient Greek myth about the fall of the city of Troy. Troy was conquered when the invading Greeks were brought into the city concealed in a large wooden horse statue. It also referred to the infiltration of the group by a law enforcement official. Group members knew this individual as Robert Gonzalez, but his real name was Robert Rodriguez.

The ATF members actually taking part in the raid had a different name for the operation. Recognizing the importance of media coverage, they called it Showtime.[5]

KING: Are you a sinner?

KORESH: Yeah, I'm a sinner.

KING: How do you sin?

KORESH: Thoughts, attitudes, feelings, emotions, breathing the air. You know, some people say I'm a sinner because I drink a beer.[4]

Breault also created bad publicity for the Davidians in the United States. He testified against the group in a child custody case in Michigan in February 1992. The Davidian mother in the case lost custody of her child to the child's non-Davidian father. According to Breault and King, there had been extensive unfavorable coverage of Koresh preaching death by suicide on Australian television and in some US media. The coverage might have caused him to call off a plan to have the Davidians commit mass suicide in April 1992. Other Davidians, however, deny there were such plans.

By the morning of February 28, 1993, the media as a whole had been primed to take a dim view of the Davidians. In their 1995 exposé *Inside the Cult*, Breault and King describe how reporters were poised and television cameras were already rolling. Both press and television reporters were already on the scene when the ATF convoy and three helicopters manned by the National Guard arrived not long after 9:30 a.m.

CHAPTER FOUR

A DEADLY CONFRONTATION

Seeing armed men advancing, Koresh opened the double door. The ATF men shouted "Police! Search warrant! Get down!" Koresh called back, "What's going on? There are women and children in here!"[1] He slammed the doors shut, but bullets were fired from outside through one door, as well as from inside through the other door. It is not clear who fired first. It is possible one of the ATF agents, assigned to silence the group's pet dogs, actually fired the first shots moments earlier. These dogs were in a pen elsewhere in the center. In any event, incoming shots wounded Perry Jones, a 64-year-old group member standing inside. The Davidians fired back in self-defense, they say, wounding an ATF agent in the left hand. A little later, reports say a group member fired on ATF agents in the gymnasium. The agents returned the fire and seriously wounded the group member in the hip and right wrist. The wounded

Agents attempted to find Koresh's bedroom by climbing to the compound's roof but were pushed back by gunfire.

man turned out to be Koresh himself. People inside the compound called 911 almost immediately, yelling for the authorities to call off the attack and stop shooting.

Throughout the day, Davidians and the ATF continued exchanging gunfire. In the first half hour or so, an ATF agent was killed. Other agents climbed ladders to the chapel roof, where they would have access to Koresh's room in order to serve his arrest warrant. The ATF agents also broke the windows to the room where the group stored its weapons. They threw in a "flash-bang" grenade designed to stun anyone inside. A group member in the room was able to fire his weapon, however, killing two ATF agents. The agents

THE MISSING DOOR

Photos of the right- and left-hand front doors to the Mount Carmel Center were taken during the long standoff after February 28. The left-hand door showed a half-dozen bullet holes that appeared to have been made by outgoing rounds fired by group members. When Koresh's lawyers saw the doors after the shoot-out, they believed most of the dozen bullet holes fired through the right-hand door were from incoming rounds fired by the ATF. The ATF maintains agents did not shoot through the door; they will not shoot if there is no identifiable target. When the siege finally ended, an armored vehicle driven by the FBI removed both doors and dragged them away from the building. By the following day, only the left-hand door was found. The right-hand door had disappeared. It was a crucial piece of evidence that could have proved whether the ATF fired on the center.

withdrew. By the time a cease-fire was arranged that night, six members of the Davidians were dead and an unknown number injured. The ATF suffered four dead and 16 wounded.[2]

The Beginning of Negotiations

Talks between the ATF and the Davidians began almost immediately following the initial volley of shots. Koresh conversed with the ATF, and Koresh's deputy Steve Schneider talked with the Waco police department. The first result of these talks was positive. Both sides agreed the safety of the children came first. As a result, four children were sent out the evening of February 28.[3] Parents of the children gave the ATF the names of relatives and friends whom they wanted to care for the children. Instead, officials sent the children to housing run by the Texas Department of Protective and Regulatory Services.

THE EXTENT OF KORESH'S WOUNDS

Just how serious Koresh's wounds really were will never be known, since he refused outside medical treatment during the siege. He was treated only by a group member who was a nurse. She stated his wounds were not serious and were healing. Yet his hip wound was serious enough to cause low blood pressure, headaches, and fevers. These kept him from communicating with government agents during many periods of the siege.

NATIONAL GUARD HELICOPTERS

The Posse Comitatus Act of 1878 forbids the use of US military forces to enforce the law in domestic civilian disturbances. However, the National Guard was increasingly used to quell just such disturbances throughout the mid-1900s. Three National Guard helicopters were supposed to serve as an observation post during the February 28 raid, but they ended up firing upon the compound, according to at least one eyewitness, and being fired upon in return. Two helicopters landed to inspect the damage. The other helicopter quickly withdrew from the action.

By 10:00 a.m. the next day, March 1, operational control of the government efforts had passed from the ATF to the FBI. The change in command took place mainly because FBI rules specified that it could not take part in operations involving a Hostage Rescue Team (HRT) unless it had overall command of the operation. A 50-man Hostage Rescue Team made up of well-trained and experienced sharpshooters had been brought in because of the number of armed group members.[4] They considered the standoff a hostage situation. Group members, however, did not consider themselves or their children as hostages. Instead they regarded themselves as more of an extended family. When interviewed a week later on a group-produced video, group members said they were free to leave but had chosen to stay. HRT members had not been trained to handle such a situation.

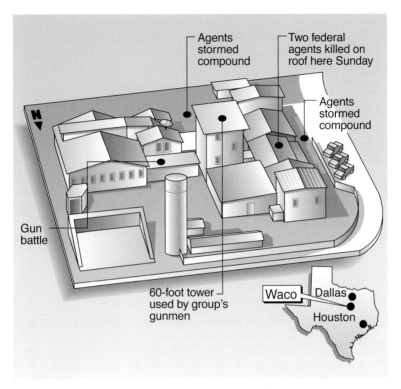

Agents attempted to enter the compound at several points.

They were used to dealing with drug dealers, cigarette smugglers, and terrorists—not a religious group trying to protect its members. A 31-man team of Texas Rangers also arrived to process the crime scene and assist the ATF and FBI.[5]

The events of March 1 looked promising when the group sent out ten children.[6] The government's stated goal was not only to secure the release of the children. They also wanted the surrender of the adult

A mixture of law enforcement groups were present at the standoff.

group members, including Koresh. In return, Koresh demanded a radio station broadcast his teachings. At 8:10 a.m. on March 2, Koresh sent out the tape he had prepared for broadcast along with two more children. Two elderly Davidian women accompanied the children.[7] The broadcast took place at 1:30 p.m. that afternoon. By 6:00 p.m., however, Koresh had changed his mind about exiting with his followers. He said God had told him to wait.

Even though Koresh had changed his mind, the standoff still seemed as if it could end with a negotiated settlement. But a fundamental distrust of each side for the other would have to be overcome. In addition, differences between the various law enforcement groups had to be resolved in order for there to be any progress.

CHAPTER
FIVE

TALK AND ACTION

As the standoff entered its third day, the FBI's strategy was plain. Its plan was to engage Koresh in conversations designed to entice more Davidians to leave. Koresh's goal, however, was quite different. He wanted to preach about the coming "end times" and the meaning of the book of Revelation. He also tried to win converts to his side. With separate concerns, both sides seemed to be talking past each other.

Negotiation vs. Physical Pressure

FBI leaders disagreed about the best way to end the standoff and gain the safe release of the approximately 100 adults and 20 children who remained in the center at the end of March 3.[1] In one camp were those who believed they could resolve the crisis by talking it through. This group consisted mostly of the negotiators, a group of 25 officials.[2] Their plan was to first create an atmosphere of openness. Then they would air their

Throughout the standoff, government officials and Davidians spoke on multiple occasions, both by telephone and at the door of the compound.

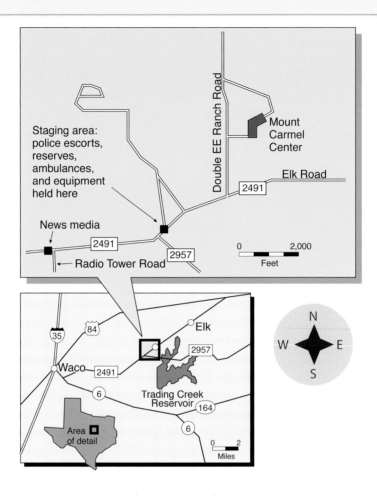

Law enforcement and the media set up command
centers at a distance from the compound.

differences and gradually reach a compromise. The
negotiators' main command post was in a hangar at a
former air force base about five miles (8 km) from the
Mount Carmel Center. The negotiators were in constant
communication with those on the scene.

Often opposed to the "talk" camp were those
inclined toward action. The 50-person HRT was trained

to use military tactics to rescue people, especially the children who they regarded as Koresh's hostages. They believed the children were in immediate danger from the group members and wanted to remove the children as quickly as possible. The talk group, however, viewed the Mount Carmel residents as a religious group practicing its beliefs, even though some of those beliefs, such as Koresh's practice of polygamy, were illegal. The people within Mount Carmel did not consider themselves as hostages. Because the negotiators understood the Branch Davidians' motivation differently than the action group, both groups came to their own conclusions about the best way to resolve the situation. The peaceful emergence of sect members arranged by the negotiators and the members themselves were often followed by "get tough" measures taken by other FBI agents to remind the Davidians who was really in control.

Promising Developments and Setbacks

Despite their differences with group members, FBI agents had some success in getting people to come out. Other government actions soon impaired the groups' trust in the negotiators, however. Members learned from a CNN broadcast the two elderly women who came out on March 2 would face attempted murder charges in the deaths of the four ATF members on February 28. The Davidians bitterly protested this news. As a result, the FBI convinced the US attorney general's office to drop the charges. Instead, they would hold the women only as witnesses. Koresh may have appreciated the FBI's action. In any case, three children left the compound from

DUELING FBI AND DAVIDIAN VIDEOS

The FBI made a film of the children who had left the center in an attempt to show the children were well cared for and hopefully persuade parents to send more children out. The films showed them happily jumping up and down on couches, eating, and drinking soda pop at will. The Davidians inside the center disapproved of the children's behavior. Yet Koresh and Schneider recognized one thing. If the public saw the film, it might create bad publicity for the Davidians. Schneider decided to make his own film of group members and their children inside the center. The resulting two-hour film shows Schneider interviewing a dozen or so group members, including one family. The film shows Judy Schneider (Steve Schneider's wife), Kathy Schroeder, the five members of the Henry family, Scott Sonobe, whose children had already left the compound, and several women from the United Kingdom, including Doris Fagan, Bernadette Monbelly, and Rosemary Morrison. The film also shows Koresh and a handful of children, many with their mothers. The group members state they came to Waco to study the Bible with Koresh. They say they came there freely and can leave any time they want.

March 3 through March 5.[3]
In an attempt to gain the release
of still more children, the FBI
sent a videotape of the released
children into the center on
March 5.

On March 7, however,
Koresh refused to consider
sending out any more children.
When asked why, he replied,
"You're dealing with my
biological children now. . . .
that's what we've come down
to."[4] Koresh was in fact the
father of at least 16 of the
children remaining in the
center.[5] He claimed Biblical justification for his exclusive
right to the women and older children of the group.
He cited (among other passages from scripture) the
Song of Solomon 6:8, which seemed to authorize the
Messiah access to "threescore queens, and foursquare
concubines, and virgins without number."[6] Koresh
believed Revelation 4:4 predicted his children would

A MELTING POT OF COUNTRIES

Before the Waco siege, approximately 130 group members were living at Mount Carmel. Most were white Americans, but many were from other countries and ethnic groups. They included 33 British (almost all of whom were of African descent); three New Zealanders (all Asian); five Australians; five Asian Americans; two Filipinos; three Canadians; one Jamaican, and one Israeli.[7] Many of those from other countries had been recruited by Koresh and Schneider on trips to Israel and Australia.

Children and group members left the compound in ones and twos throughout March.

reign in the new kingdom. Critics cited evidence Koresh had illegal sex with girls as young as 12.

One Step Forward, Two Steps Back

By March 12, the FBI team of negotiators had made some more progress. At 10:41 that morning, group member Kathy Schroeder left the center. She had lost her husband in the February 28 shoot-out and had previously sent out her children. Group member Oliver Gyarfas left the center. A medical team also made calls into the center, offering medical advice and treatment to two wounded individuals inside. Both Scott Sonobe and Judy Schneider, who had been wounded in the February 28 assault, spoke to a medical doctor. However, they refused to come out for treatment. That evening, a video showing Schroeder's reunion with her three-year-old son, Bryan, was sent into the center in hopes it would persuade others with children on the outside to leave. There was no immediate response.

That same night, FBI special agent in charge (SAC) Jeffrey Jamar shut off electricity to the center. He said he "wanted those inside the compound to experience the same wet and cold night as the tactical personnel outside."[8] Koresh and Steve Schneider bitterly criticized the action. Some of the negotiators also disagreed with the decision. SAC Jamar's strategy was to drive a wedge between Koresh and his supporters. Some negotiators, however, thought this strategy prevented them from establishing credibility with those in the complex.

Both Koresh and Schneider were still angry and complaining about the electricity shutoff the next morning, March 13. They said three other group members who had been ready to come out would probably not do so now, even though they were cold and freezing. The negotiators could only blame "their bosses" for the situation and plead with Koresh and Schneider to continue their discussions.[9] Yet the electricity would not be turned back on for the rest of the siege. In addition, beginning on March 14, the FBI began shining bright lights on the center to disrupt members' sleep. The lighting also provided better security for the HRT, which was on duty around the clock. In another modification of their strategy for resolving the standoff, the negotiators decided to continue focusing on achieving a peaceful solution but would not listen to any more "Bible babble," as they called it.[10]

A Meeting of Minds

Despite the hard feelings from the previous two days, March 15 produced an unusual defusing of emotions on both sides. Negotiators called for a meeting of four people: FBI negotiator Byron Sage; Jack Harwell, the local sheriff, who knew several members; Schneider, Koresh's deputy; and Wayne Martin, a group member and attorney who had represented many local residents in court. The four met in the driveway approximately 50 yards (46 m) from the center. Schneider said God had told Koresh to stay inside but the others were free to leave at any time. Sage and Harwell were successfully able to address several items of concern. These included the Davidians' right to counsel, the availability of medical attention, and the need to preserve the crime scene.

The week of March 12 to March 19 ended on an upbeat note. The FBI delivered materials to the center that included an audiotape from a theologian, a letter from the Christian Broadcasting Network, and a statement from the US attorney general's office. The statement guaranteed the government would not seek legal means to take over the land on which the Mount Carmel Center stood. Schneider was pleased. He told negotiator Sage more members would soon exit.

SHERIFF JACK HARWELL

Because he knew many of the group members outside the context of the siege, Sheriff Jack Harwell was in a position to see them as real people, not just illustrations of stereotypical "religious nuts." Harwell smoothed the way for the FBI to deliver milk for the children in the center. Survivor David Thibodeau's mother characterized Harwell as a "typical live-and-let-live Texan. He felt [group members] ought to have been left alone, but he had to bow to the feds [federal agents]."[11]

CHAPTER
SIX

TENSIONS BUILD

Each of the parties in the standoff—law enforcement officials and group members—and their respective leaders tried to control the situation to their advantage. But each party also needed to minimize internal tensions in order to present a united front to the other side.

During the siege, the FBI permitted almost 100 contacts between group members inside the center and family members outside. On March 20 and 21 alone, 13 different telephone calls, relayed messages, or tape recordings went into or out of the center.[1] On March 20, the FBI allowed released Davidian Brad Branch to make a telephone call from outside to Schneider and Koresh. On March 21, the FBI passed in tape recordings by Kathy Schroeder (to her friends inside the center) and by Oliver Gyarfas (to his sister Aisha).

The FBI's purpose in allowing these contacts was to pressure Koresh into allowing more group members to leave the center. Yet those who remained behind seemed

Group members who left the compound attended a March 22 hearing at the Waco federal courthouse.

to accept their discomforts as a test of their beliefs. Sheila Martin left her husband Wayne behind and took her three children out of the center on March 21. The FBI allowed Sheila to call her husband shortly after she left. Sheila told him she and the kids were doing well, but Wayne replied, "Time is short, and God is angry."[2]

David Thibodeau said the whole siege experience gave him "a sense of going beyond the boundaries of everyday existence . . . into another, more exalted realm."[3] Group members often referred to the outside world (and the US government in particular) as Babylon. Babylon is described in Bible passages including chapter 17 of the book of Revelation as a place of materialism, luxury, and evil. Koresh probably released some group members back into this world as a punishment for being troublemakers. In any case, none of the group members contacted from the outside during the period of March 21 to 27 left the center. The FBI's attempts to open cracks between the Branch Davidians were not working.

Outward Opposites: David Koresh and Steve Schneider

High school dropout Koresh and college-educated university lecturer Schneider could not have appeared more outwardly different. The Bible-quoting Koresh demanded allegiance by the sheer force of his good looks and commanding personality. Schneider was less fiery, though no less articulate. Although he was described as Koresh's deputy and second in command, Schneider never sought a public leadership role. A key player behind the scenes, he was

DAVIDIAN DEMANDS AND FBI RESPONSES

During the entire siege, group members made 41 separate demands of the FBI. These demands included requests for milk, writing materials, magazines, the playing of tapes on local and national media, turning on the electricity, and so on. The FBI granted 25 of the demands, such as requests for writing materials, and denied 16, including demands for media contacts.[5] However, the items were not granted entirely freely: the plastic milk jugs contained listening devices so the FBI could spy inside the compound. Group members continued requesting milk for the children even after they discovered the devices.

usually content to act as a spokesperson and messenger for Koresh's demands. This division of duties seemed to help both men work together, as did their common belief system.

Special agent Sage, however, had some doubts about how harmonious Schneider's relationship with Koresh really was. He remembered that after his apparently successful meeting with Schneider, Martin, and Sheriff

THE RELIGIOUS JOURNEY OF STEVE SCHNEIDER

Steve Schneider grew up in Wisconsin. His mother was a member of the SDA. Schneider was always in search of religious truth. He was expelled from an SDA college in England for getting drunk, but he continued his religious search, reading about different religions. Schneider met Judy Peterson in Wisconsin in approximately 1970. Peterson converted to Adventism, and the two married in 1981. Steve continued his religious studies after the two moved to Hawaii. He received a degree in comparative religion at the University of Hawaii while working as a teaching assistant. Then in 1986, Schneider met Koresh through Marc Breault while Koresh was on a recruitment trip to Hawaii. Despite having some doubts about Koresh, Schneider eventually decided Koresh was the Messiah after seeing him debate a professor in California. Although Schneider aspired to be an evangelist himself, he realized his own powers as such did not compare with Koresh's: "It's like I sold them a toothbrush and he comes along and sells the house that goes with [the] toothbrush."[6]

Harwell on March 15, Koresh nevertheless canceled a proposed follow-up meeting. Sage concluded Koresh probably doubted the abilities of his second in command. Sage's assessment of Koresh and Schneider's relationship was missing one key fact that further complicated the situation. Schneider's wife Judy, with whom he had been unable to have a child, was also one of Koresh's wives in the polygamous group. Furthermore, Judy and Koresh had a daughter, Mayanah, of whom Steve was reportedly quite fond.

Tensions for the Negotiators

Throughout the siege, negotiators and Davidian leaders continued operating under different principles, despite sometimes seeming to agree. In two hours of conversations that ended at 11:30 p.m. on March 20, Schneider told negotiators two more elderly women might soon leave the center. Forty-five minutes later the two women appeared. A day later, FBI negotiators asked when Koresh himself would leave the center. Koresh's answer was, "I told you my God says to wait. Actually I asked for it." When a negotiator asked why he had made such a request, Koresh replied, "Because I didn't want Him to destroy you."[7] As Koresh was being

"MY GOD SAYS TO WAIT"

Koresh's statement refers to Revelation 6:9–11. This passage describes the opening of the Fifth Seal by the Lamb of God, which symbolizes Christ. Each of the Seven Seals reveals an apocalyptic event. The writer of Revelation predicted these events would happen at the end of the world. The opening of the Fifth Seal reveals the souls of those slain for preaching the word of God. These souls cry out for God to avenge their deaths. Yet they are told to wait until more such preachers are slain. Then God can avenge them all at once.

guided by the Bible and what he believed God was telling him, the FBI's psychologists were having trouble understanding his mindset and predicting his next moves.

The conflict between the FBI tactical team, which favored action, and the negotiators, who favored talk, continued throughout the siege. For example, on March 21, seven adults left the center, which the negotiators took to be a sign of progress. Yet the FBI responded that evening with two actions that infuriated negotiators as well as those remaining inside.

First, the FBI removed automobiles from the front yard of the center, damaging some in the process. Second, they played very loud music over the public address system. After asking several times that the music be turned off, Schneider angrily conveyed a message from an equally angry Koresh: "Because of the loud music,

The long standoff was wearying law enforcement officials.

nobody is coming out."[8] The next morning, March 22, Schneider remained angry about the disturbance, and there was no further contact until that evening.

At 8:27 p.m. on March 22, the FBI made a new offer to Schneider. Koresh and the remaining group members could communicate with each other and hold religious services while in jail. Koresh would also be permitted to make a worldwide broadcast on the Christian Broadcasting Network. Koresh rejected the offer the following morning.

During the day, Jamar had called a meeting to discuss various "stress escalation measures" that might be introduced if there were no further positive responses to FBI requests.[9] This was the first meeting at which the negotiators

TOUGH TALK

Both the tactical team's actions and the negotiators' talk could be very aggressive. On March 17, for example, Sage told Koresh over the phone the leader's earlier promise to come out if the FBI could solve the puzzle of the Seven Seals in the book of Revelation was "garbage." Sage said he himself knew from the Bible only the Lamb of God could unlock the seals. Apparently Sage did not know Koresh had already said he, Koresh, was really the Lamb. Furthermore, Sage said he knew he was among the saved, and Koresh had no right to judge him. Taken aback, Koresh from then on referred respectfully to Sage as "Mr. Byron."[10] However, Sage later commented, "You don't want to debate theology with somebody who believes they are Christ. You're never going to win."[11]

recommended tear gas be used to resolve the crisis if other measures did not work. The team that had once favored "talk" was now beginning to prepare their next moves if Koresh continued delaying his surrender.

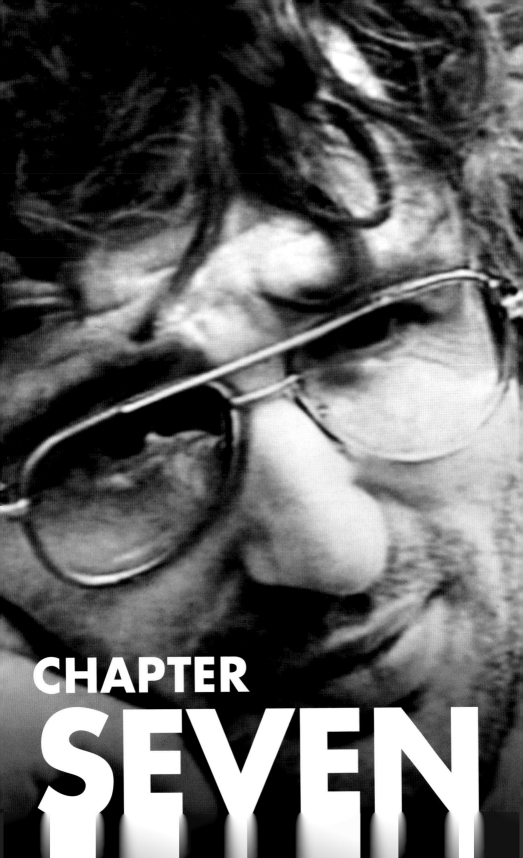

CHAPTER
SEVEN

LIVING FAITH OR FALSE RELIGION?

Conversations between FBI negotiators and Koresh and Schneider, as well as their lawyers and other group members, continued until almost the end of the standoff. Most contacts during this period were through phone conversations. The negotiators tried two approaches. First, they attempted to get a pledge from Koresh to send out a certain number of people. Second, they tried to get a specific date on which all group members would promise to leave the center. When the response to either request was specific, negotiators pressed for details to confirm it was also sincere. When the response was vague or negative, the FBI would threaten an unspecified action.

For example, at 1:13 p.m. on March 25, a negotiator gave Schneider until 4:00 p.m. to send out at least ten to 20 people or face "certain actions."[1] Nothing happened by 4:00. The FBI then began using armored vehicles

Law enforcement officials had trouble understanding Koresh's religion and his relationship with his followers.

to remove a number of motorcycles and children's go-carts from the front yard of the center. The FBI made similar demands for the next two days. The first time, Schneider's only reaction was to complain and start preaching from the book of Revelation. The second time, Schneider said "You can burn us down, kill us, whatever," but no one wanted to come out.[2]

Jamar decided to let both Koresh and Schneider have face-to-face meetings with their attorneys, Dick

THE BABYLON CONNECTION

Following the book of Revelation, Branch Davidians called the outside world Babylon. Group members regularly entered that world, whether to work or to shop. Yet they still regarded this Babylon as a totally separate and materialistic, secular, and sinful place. The actual Babylonian kingdom dated from the time of Hammurabi, approximately 1750 BCE. In 587 BCE, the city of Jerusalem, capital of the Jewish kingdom, fell to the Babylonians. Large numbers of Jews, including the prophet Ezekiel, were deported to Babylon. It was not until almost 50 years later, in 539, that Cyrus the Great, King of the Persians, captured Babylon. Cyrus allowed the Jews to return to Jerusalem and resume their worship. King Cyrus's favor toward the Jews gave them the means and confidence to rebuild their religious and national identity. For his actions, the book of Isaiah hailed Cyrus as Messiah, or "God's anointed." Koresh named his first son Cyrus. Perhaps Koresh hoped Cyrus would someday bring similar power to the Davidians.

DeGuerin and Jack Zimmerman respectively. Jamar's decision may have let Koresh feel as if he had more control of the situation than he actually did. Jamar still wanted to end the conflict peacefully. More than 30 hours of talks took place between March 29 and April 14, mostly between Koresh and DeGuerin.

Because of attorney-client privilege, these meetings were not recorded. Some had to do with setting a time for leaving the compound. Koresh kept changing the conditions for surrender. First, he said he would leave at the end of Passover, which would have been April 12. Then he extended that date until April 14. On April 14, however, Koresh stated a new condition. He said he would come out only after he finished writing his explanation of the Seven Seals. The FBI saw these delays as a stalling

THE DAVIDIANS' LAWYER

The youthful-looking, 52-year-old Mercedes-driving DeGuerin was "easily the second-most well-known criminal defense attorney in Texas," according to Texas journalist Dick Reavis.[3] DeGuerin devised a plan that would pay Koresh's legal fees from the proceeds of Koresh's memoirs. Any additional profits would go to a trust fund set up to benefit Koresh's children. A literary agent estimated the memoirs could bring in as much as $2.5 million dollars.

tactic. The Davidians, however, supported their leader's spiritual goal.

The Seven Seals

The book of Revelation contains John's vision of being carried up to heaven and seeing the scroll sealed with the Seven Seals. This is one of the most mystical and powerful scenes in the Bible. Scholars have long debated the meaning of the symbols in this story. The key images of the Seven Seals begin with a mysterious figure sitting on a throne. The figure is surrounded by four living creatures and a scroll. The figures are a glorified lion, an ox, a human, and an eagle-like bird (Rev. 4:2, 7). An angel asks if anyone can open and read the scroll (5:2). John weeps because there is no response to the question. A nearby elder comforts John. The elder says, "Do not weep! See, the Lion of the tribe of Judah, the Root of David, has triumphed. He is able to open the scroll and its

THE FIRST FOUR SEALS

Seal One is a white horse with a rider who wears a crown and a bow (Rev. 6:1–2). Seal Two is a bright red horse whose rider has a sword that lets him "take peace from the earth" (6:4). Seal Three is a black horse whose rider has a balance scale and who seems to be selling food (6:5). Seal Four is a pale horse ridden by a figure whose name is Death (6:6).

Group members hung a banner from a window listing Bible verse citations, including a reference to the first of the Seven Seals.

seven seals" (5:5). Then John sees a lamb standing, as if slain. The lamb takes the scroll from the seated figure on the throne (5:8). As the lamb opens each seal, a vision appears.

As a result of a religious experience he had in 1985 in Israel, Koresh identified himself as that lamb. He believed his group was now living out the events predicted in the Fifth Seal. "The souls of them that were slain for [preaching] the word of God" (Rev. 6:9) cry out for revenge. God tells them to "rest yet for a little season" (6:11). Then they too will die before being resurrected among the chosen. Cued by the Sixth Seal, Koresh predicted an earthquake would strike Waco. "I forewarn you, the Lake Waco area of Old Mount Carmel will be terribly shaken. The waters of the lake will be emptied through the broken dam."[4] Koresh made this prediction in a letter to DeGuerin on April 14. Finally, the Seventh Seal describes the destruction of Earth and almost its entire population. The only people to be saved would be 144,000 chosen people. They alone would enjoy the Second Coming of Christ, and the creation of a new heaven and a new Earth. For the Davidians, this was the heart of the matter. As Koresh wrote in his manuscript on the book of Revelation, "All the books of the Bible begin and end in Revelation."[5] For many of the negotiators, however, it

KORESH'S ACADEMIC INTERPRETERS

Koresh desired a chance to debate Bible scholars over the meaning of the seals. He knew if scholars were won to his side, they could spread his message more quickly. Dr. James Tabor and his colleague, Dr. Philip Arnold, wanted to engage with Koresh in order to hopefully prevent more violence. Neither was allowed to speak directly to Koresh. However, they persuaded a local television talk show host to present their work on the Seven Seals. The group saw the broadcast but did not agree with the academics' interpretation. Tabor later published Koresh's unfinished manuscript explaining the First Seal.

was just another example of the "Bible babble" they had, a month earlier, resolved to ignore.

To the FBI, if Koresh was not putting off his inevitable defeat, then he was simply talking nonsense. When theologian Philip Arnold offered to explain to the FBI what Koresh was saying about the seals, FBI spokesperson Robert Ricks responded, "There is nobody who can understand what this man [Koresh] is saying."[6] Koresh was only able to complete his written explanation of the first and second seals before events overtook him. That explanation was put on a computer disc and brought out of Mount Carmel on April 19 by Koresh's secretary, Ruth Riddle. By then, the "little season" of time Koresh had requested had almost run out.

KORESH'S SECRETARY

One of the siege's survivors, Ruth Riddle, was the secretary who transcribed Koresh's work on the first and second seals. Riddle broke her ankle, but she managed to bring out the computer disk containing the chapter on the First Seal when the standoff was finally broken on April 19.

CHAPTER
EIGHT

APOCALYPSE NOW

J ust before 6:00 a.m. on April 19, 1993, FBI special agent Sage phoned into the complex and announced tear gas was about to be introduced. He noted this was not an assault. Sage said no FBI agents would enter the complex. He asked that no weapons be fired. Sage then got on the loudspeaker. He advised those inside to come out, as they were now under arrest. Two Combat Engineering Vehicles (CEVs) started injecting gas into some buildings at 6:02 a.m. Two minutes later the Davidians opened fire on the CEVs.

Skipping the Small Print

Before Reno approved the tear gas plan on April 18, she asked for a written statement from the FBI documenting everything it proposed to do. According to the official *Report to the Deputy Attorney General*, released by the Justice Department in October 1993, however, Reno "did not read the prepared statement carefully, nor did she read the supporting documentation" itself.[1] The

The military vehicles that had surrounded the compound for days were ready to move in the morning of April 19.

statement said if the FBI were fired upon, the agency was then authorized immediately to use Bradley Fighting Vehicles (BVs) to shoot containers of tear gas through the windows of the entire complex. The FBI was also authorized to fire back if fired upon. The agency maintains, however, that FBI agents never fired a shot during the entire 51-day operation.

One crucial detail involved in using BVs was known only to FBI veterans and chemists. The BVs used a different kind of tear gas than the CEVs, called CS. The tear gas powder sprayed by the CEVs was suspended in harmless carbon dioxide. The powder in the containers

BVs AND CEVs

At Waco, the BVs removed obstacles and debris from the open areas surrounding the complex and enabled government agents to move around open areas without danger of being shot. Each BV had its weapons removed to make it primarily a defensive vehicle. A BV carries a team of seven.

CEVs provide combat support for ground troops and vehicles. They carry a crew of four and are heavier than BVs. The five CEVs at Waco were used to remove obstacles and debris. The CEVs' primary purpose was to punch holes in the building and inject tear gas using a long boom. Once government forces came under fire, however, BVs were used to shoot tear gas containers because they could do it faster and more safely for the vehicle operators.

delivered by BVs, however, was suspended in poisonous methylene chloride. The *Army Field Manual FM0-21-27* warns, "When using the dry agent CS-1, do not discharge indoors. Accumulated dust may explode when exposed to spark or open flame."[2]

Beginning at 6:07 a.m., BVs began deploying the more dangerous type of gas. By 6:31 a.m., the HRT reported filling the entire center with gas. Yet CEVs and BVs continued delivering gas into the center. In the process, CEVs broke through the main building's walls twice at approximately 7:58 a.m. This action created large holes in both the front and the back-right corner of the structure. These holes, and a third one in the rear near the gymnasium, were soon expanded to make it easier for those wishing to escape the complex to leave. As the CEVs and BVs became more aggressive in their movements, however, the debris they created ended up

TEAR GAS

The CS type of tear gas causes irritation not only of the eyes but also of the skin and respiratory system. According to a US Army manual, tear gas can make persons "incapable of executing organized and concerted actions. . . . Excessive exposure to [tear gas] can make them incapable of vacating the area."[3] If burned, it can give off deadly fumes, says one of its manufacturers. It can also catch fire if present in large amounts.

Tanks punched holes in the compound's walls in order to let the tear gas in and group members out.

blocking other exits with which group members were more familiar.

Running Out of Gas

For 90 minutes, the FBI shot tear gas into the complex. By then, the agency had nearly run out of the rounds it had on hand. Forty-eight more rounds were rushed to Mount Carmel.[4] The BVs continued to shoot tear gas into the complex. Yet by 10:00 a.m., no one had exited. To complicate matters further, high winds of up to

35 miles per hour (56 kmh) began blowing away large amounts of the gas. It looked as though the siege might go on.

Reno used the slow pace of the operation as a reason to leave for a speaking engagement in Baltimore, Maryland, at 11:30 a.m. In the meantime, FBI agents realized the phone line into the complex was broken. Phone contact with the complex was never restored. FBI agents were reluctant to risk being fired upon in order to fix the phone line. The line ran under the fully exposed front yard of the main building.

The Fire

A fire broke out on the second floor of the dormitory at 12:07 p.m. Time stamps on images taken by a forward looking infrared (FLIR) camera in an overhead plane recorded the time. The images also

EFFECTS OF TEAR GAS ON CHILDREN

Professor of law and psychiatry Dr. Alan A. Stone was hired by the government to review law enforcement actions at Waco during the standoff. Stone concluded tear gas should not have been used. Stone posed basic questions about the danger the gas posed to the 21 children 15 years old or younger in the complex, of whom approximately a dozen were under the age of eight. He felt the information presented to Attorney General Reno downplayed the known risks of the gas. Stone concluded use of the gas threatened rather than protected the children's health and safety.

Fire engulfed the compound with many group members still inside.

showed two other fires breaking out at almost the same time. Investigators considered the suspicious timing an almost sure sign of two or more arsonists at work. In addition, an HRT member says he saw a group member starting a fire on the front side of the building. Later statements by Branch Davidians referred to overhearing other group members saying things such as "Start the fires" and "The fire has been lit."[5] Fire had religious significance for the Branch Davidians and was associated with end times.

Critics of the execution of the tear gas plan claim the first fire actually started at 11:59 a.m. This was one interpretation of flashes shown on the FLIR camera in the overhead plane. The camera placed the fire in the gymnasium right after a CEV backed out of the room. These critics of the arson theory say the tank somehow created the fatal spark that started the fire. These critics believe the hole the tank knocked in the gym wall also served as a flue, pushing the fire swiftly through the building. A national arson team, however, later concluded the FBI's actions did not cause the fire. Mere minutes after the first FLIR sighting of a fire, the entire complex was engulfed. Fire trucks arrived at the scene at 12:34 p.m. but were held back for seven minutes because of the danger of gunfire. HRT agents entered the main building while it was burning to look for trapped survivors but found no one to rescue.

Much of the Mount Carmel Center burned to the ground.

Negotiators broadcast messages over loudspeakers asking people to come out, but few did.

To Live or Die

At 12:18 p.m. the first of nine survivors, Renos Avraam, jumped off the second story roof and was taken into custody. A woman came out through a doorway with her clothes on fire. Yet when she saw FBI vehicles, she tried to reenter the burning building and had to be stopped by HRT agents. Misty Ferguson, age 17, was running toward a window to jump out when the floor collapsed beneath her. She held out her hands to break her fall, but her fingers and thumbs were burnt off. Ruth Riddle jumped off the second story roof and broke her ankle. Four of the male survivors, Clive Doyle, Jaime Castillo, Derek Lovelock, and David Thibodeau, escaped through the front right section of the building. The last survivor, Graeme Craddock, came out approximately three hours after the fire's start. He had been holed up in a concrete room near the water tower. According to reporter Peter Boyer, it took a week before the charred remains of the center were cool enough to be examined closely.

"Now I'm down on my hands and knees, praying, *God, if I'm going to die just make it quick.* Just then, the wall of the stage [in the chapel] catches fire, scorching the side of my face. The sharp smell of singed hair fills my nostrils and I scream from the depths of my gut. Seeing Jaime and Derek [two other survivors] run out of the hole in the wall at the edge of the stage, I follow, preferring a swift death by the agents' bullets to being roasted by fire."[6]
—David Thibodeau, sect member and one of nine survivors of the fire on April 19, 1993

Clive Doyle survived the April 19 fire at Mount Carmel. After, he organized memorials and became a spokesperson for survivors.

The FBI recovered 75 bodies. Of these, 32 died of smoke and carbon monoxide inhalation. Seventeen died of gunshot wounds that had the marks of either suicide or mercy killing. Nine died of suffocation, nine of burns, and three of blunt force trauma caused by falling masonry. The remaining three died from a variety of known and unknown causes. Twenty-six of the dead were under the age of 18, but some ages had to be estimated because of the lack of dental records.[7] A later report on the day's events stated five of these minors had been shot by Davidians.[8]

Koresh and Schneider both died in the telephone room of gunshot wounds. Koresh's wound was to the forehead, Schneider's to the mouth. Their wives Rachel Koresh and Judy Schneider were both buried alive when the main building collapsed; they died of suffocation.

The siege at Waco was over, but the consequences for the remaining Davidians were only beginning. The lessons to be learned from the tragedy are still being debated today.

CHAPTER
NINE

THE AFTERMATH

T hirty-five people left the center before the fire, and another nine survived it.[1] Twelve were charged with crimes committed sometime during the siege. One of the accused, Kathy Schroeder, later pleaded guilty to all charges. She then agreed to testify against the remaining 11 defendants. There were three main charges against them. Count one was "conspiracy to murder federal officers." Count two was "aiding and abetting the murder of federal officers." Count three was "using a firearm during a crime of violence."[2]

The Verdict for the Waco 11

On February 26, 1994, a jury found all 11 remaining defendants not guilty of count one. Three defendants, Clive Doyle, Norman Allison, and Woodrow Kendrick, were found innocent of all charges. Seven defendants were guilty of count two. Five of those seven were also guilty of count three. Two defendants, Paul Fatta and

The US flag and the ATF flag flew above the ruins as investigators began searching for victims and evidence.

Graeme Craddock, were guilty of other weapons charges.

Because of a fault in the instructions to the jury, Judge Walter S. Smith Jr. decided to drop count three. As a result, the jury verdict should have led to an average sentence of several years each. At sentencing, however, Judge Smith went back on his decision to drop count three. Instead, he imposed long sentences for eight of the defendants. The Davidians appealed the ruling. On June 4, 2000, the US Supreme Court reduced four group members' sentences by 25 years, and another group member's sentence by five years. By July 2007, seven years later, all 12 defendants were free.

Timothy McVeigh's bomb destroyed an entire side of the Alfred Murrah Federal Building.

Shifting Public Opinion

Public opinion and the mainstream media at first supported Attorney General Reno. They defended the government response to the Branch Davidians' actions. Reno in particular received praise for taking full responsibility for the government's response. As the details of the tragedy began to sink in, however, public opinion began shifting. The Oklahoma City bombing in 1995 took place two years to the day after the Waco disaster. Timothy McVeigh, the mastermind of the bombing, said it was an act of revenge for the government's actions at Waco. The bombing killed 168 people.[3] A federal jury sentenced McVeigh to death by lethal injection for his crime. Yet the connection to Waco kept interest in the 1993 disaster alive.

In 1997, the documentary *Waco: The Rules of Engagement* won an Emmy. The movie was critical of some law enforcement tactics during the siege. It suggested the FBI used pyrotechnic devices that started the fire and then concealed their use for years. The film also charged that the FBI shot and killed group members attempting to flee the fire. The FBI and a special arson investigation group had already denied these charges in the 1993 Justice Department report. By August 1999, a *Time* magazine survey found 61 percent of those polled believed government agents were responsible for starting the deadly fire.[4]

The Danforth Report

Reno asked former Senator John C. Danforth to investigate the charge that the FBI had used pyrotechnic rounds of tear gas on the day of the siege. Danforth issued his final report on July 20, 2000. He found the rounds of tear gas in question did not start the fire. Danforth's report drew three additional conclusions.

First, the FBI did not shoot at Branch Davidians on April 19. Second, they did not improperly use the US military. Third, the government did not engage in a conspiracy and cover-up. Instead, Danforth placed responsibility for the tragedy solely with certain Branch Davidians and their leader. However, critics found inconsistencies between the government reports and argued that Danforth's report had merely defended the government rather than getting to the truth of the events.

The Waco debate now takes place largely on the Internet. Conspiracy theorists and those who distrust the government argue law enforcement botched the operation or even caused the tragedy on purpose. However, many people agree with FBI negotiator Sage. They firmly believe the FBI did everything it could to avoid loss of life. Yet in an interview on ABC News in 2003, Sage made a confession, admitting the government

SENATOR DANFORTH

John Danforth served 26 years in public office, including 18 years as a senator from Missouri. Beginning in September 1999, he served a year as special counsel to Reno, investigating the Waco raid. His staff interviewed more than 1,000 witnesses, pored over 2.3 million pages of documents, and examined thousands of pounds of physical evidence.[5]

had underestimated how much control Koresh had over his followers. Sage's final assessment: "I honestly feel this would have ended tragically no matter what."[6]

Reflections of Waco Survivors

Since the event, many Waco survivors and people with ties to the Branch Davidians have written about their experiences. Professor Catherine Wessinger of Loyola University has worked with survivors Clive Doyle and Sheila Martin and with Koresh's mother to publish their accounts. Survivor David Thibodeau, aided by writer Leon Whiteson, has left a very complete record of his life before, during, and after the Waco siege. Thibodeau first came to know David Koresh in 1990 as a fellow rock musician in California. The conclusion of his book, *A Place Called Waco*, expresses the feelings of many survivors toward the Davidian community:

> I'm still making mistakes, but I'm not going to let those errors destroy my self-respect. While striving to knit up

Mourners raised a memorial to Koresh and his followers near the ruined Mount Carmel Center. A tree was also planted in memory of each person who died.

the loose strands of my nature, I go on drumming and witnessing, doing what I can to honor the hard truths David Koresh, my friend and teacher, and the community he created gave me as a gift.[8]

Others, however, especially those who left the center before the fatal fire, sometimes reach the conclusion drawn by defector Marc Breault. Breault was a close

PREVENTING ANOTHER WACO

Scholars have studied the Waco siege to try to prevent a similar tragedy from occurring. Jayne Docherty, a professor at the Center for Justice and Peacebuilding at Eastern Mennonite University, offers several ideas that might lessen such conflicts in the future. For example:

- Develop other terms besides *hostages* to describe religious group members who consider themselves willing subjects of their leader.
- "Develop a new [method] for crisis negotiation" between groups that do not share common mainstream worldviews. To the Davidians, for example, CEVs and BVs

did not represent legitimate authority. Rather, the tanks confirmed their belief they were indeed in "end times." They believed the evil powers of Babylon were testing their faith.

- The Davidians might have responded better to a less aggressive approach. The ATF felt justified to "*force* [emphasis in original] the community out of their sacred space." The alternative would have been to understand the Davidians recognized only their own space and authority.
- Try to correct the biased views of many people, in which alternative religious groups are perceived "cults."[9]

friend of both Steven Schneider and his wife Judy. He left the center in September 1989 when Koresh said he wanted Breault's newly wedded wife to have sexual relations only with Koresh. As he explained in his memoir, *Inside the Cult:*

> I want to show people what we went through, so they won't make the same mistakes we did, and so the damned ruins of that fortress [the Mount Carmel Center] won't be a monument to anything, except evil.[10]

Thibodeau's statement reflects the respect the great majority of the Branch Davidians felt for their leader. Breault's statement reflects more the attitude of many outsiders. These outsiders were not comfortable with Koresh's beliefs about the end times and his uncommon definitions of marriage and morality. Those who can see the Waco tragedy from both Thibodeau's and Breault's different points of view can perhaps best understand its full meaning.

TIMELINE

1959
David Koresh is born as Vernon Howell on August 17.

1981
Koresh arrives at Mount Carmel and is hired as a repairman.

ca. 1984
Koresh marries 14-year-old Rachel Jones.

1984
Koresh's group leaves Mount Carmel for Palestine, Texas.

1988
Koresh moves with his followers back to Mount Carmel, pays off the center's back taxes, and takes control of the Davidians.

1992
In May, a suspicious package addressed to the Davidians breaks open on delivery, setting the stage for an ATF raid the following February.

1993

Six Davidians and four ATF agents are killed, and others wounded, in a shoot-out at Mount Carmel on February 28.

1993

On March 7, Koresh says the children remaining in the compound are his, and he will not release them.

1993

On March 12, Janet Reno is sworn in as attorney general of the United States; power is turned off at the center for the rest of the siege.

1993

The FBI begins lighting up the complex with bright lights at night on March 14.

1993

Steve Schneider, Wayne Martin, FBI negotiator Byron Sage, and Sheriff Jack Harwell meet outside the center and discuss many issues of concern on March 15.

TIMELINE

1993
On March 21, the FBI begins playing very loud music over the public address system at night.

1993
The FBI first considers using tear gas to break the Waco siege on March 22.

1993
On March 29, Koresh and Schneider begin series of meetings with their lawyers.

1993
The tear gas plan is presented to Attorney General Reno on April 12.

1993
On April 18, Reno notifies President Bill Clinton she has approved the tear gas plan.

1993
On April 19, 75 Davidians, including Koresh and 26 children, die in the tear gas operation and fire.

1994
On February 26, a federal district jury finds all Davidian defendants not guilty of conspiring to murder federal officers. Eight are found guilty of other charges.

1994
On June 17, Judge Walter Smith Jr. changes the jury's February decision. He sentences the eight convicted defendants to an average of 30 years in prison.

2007
By July, all 12 defendants are free.

ESSENTIAL FACTS

Date of Event
February 28–April 19, 1993

Place of Event
Waco, Texas

Key Players
- David Koresh

- Steve Schneider

- Jeffrey Jamar

- Janet Reno

- Walter S. Smith Jr.

Highlights of Event
- ATF agents raided the Davidian community at the Mount Carmel Center on February 28, 1993, in an attempt to serve search and arrest warrants. Six ATF agents and four Davidians were killed, setting off a 51-day siege. Thirty-five Davidians were released during the siege, including 21 children, but more than 80 people remained inside. The vast majority either chose to stay or were convinced to do so by David Koresh, the leader of the group.

- A plan to gradually inject tear gas was intended to force out the remaining group members. A fire swept through the compound; it is unclear how it started. The resulting blaze quickly destroyed the highly flammable center. Nine group members escaped alive. The remaining Davidians died of a variety of causes, including asphyxiation, gunshot wounds, burns, and blunt force trauma caused by falling debris.

- In 1994, eight Davidians were sentenced to prison for crimes committed during the siege. None, however, was convicted of any conspiracy or murder charge. The sentences were greatly reduced in 2000 under a US Supreme Court ruling. By 2007, all convicted Davidians were free.

Quote

"I honestly feel this would have ended tragically no matter what." —*Byron Sage, FBI negotiator*

GLOSSARY

affidavit
A sworn statement made to a judge or magistrate.

allegation
A statement that is not supported by evidence.

anecdotal
Based on or consisting of reports or observations of usually unscientific observers.

apocalyptic
Of or relating to the end of the world.

automatic weapon
A firearm that will fire repeatedly, until the trigger is released.

defector
A person who forsakes one group for another.

escalation
The state of expanding or increasing by stages.

infiltrate
To enter unobtrusively.

jurisdiction
The limit or territory in which a law enforcement group can operate.

legitimate
In accordance with the law.

materialism
A way of thinking that gives too much importance to material comforts at the expense of the spiritual and natural side of life.

polygamist
A person who has more than one wife or husband at the same time.

pyrotechnic
Related to a device used to produce an explosion.

secular
Not religious or sacred; worldly.

tactical
Of or relating to small-scale actions serving a larger purpose.

warrant
A document issued by a court that gives the police the power to do something.

ADDITIONAL RESOURCES

Selected Bibliography

Breault, Marc, and Martin King. *Inside the Cult.* New York, Signet, 1993. Print.

Linedecker, Clifford L. *Massacre at Waco, Texas.* New York: St. Martin's, 1993. Print.

Reavis, Dick J. *The Ashes of Waco: An Investigation.* New York: Simon, 1995. Print.

Report to the Deputy Attorney General on the Events at Waco, Texas February 28 to April 19, 1993. Redacted Version. *US Department of Justice.* 8 Oct. 1993. Web. 27 Aug. 2013.

Thibodeau, David, and Leon Whiteson. *A Place Called Waco: A Survivor's Story.* New York: Public Affairs, 1999. Print.

Further Readings

Cowan, Douglas E., and David G. Bromley. *Cults and New Religions: A Brief History.* Malden, MA: Blackwell, 2008. Print.

Treanor, Nick, ed. *The Waco Standoff.* Farmington Hills, MI: Greenhaven, 2003. Print.

Web Sites

To learn more about the Waco standoff,
visit ABDO Publishing Company online at
www.abdopublishing.com. Web sites about the Waco
standoff are featured on our Book Links page. These links
are routinely monitored and updated to provide the most
current information available.

Places to Visit

Helen Marie Taylor Museum
701 Jefferson Ave
Waco, TX 76701
254-752-4774
This museum, open by appointment only, features exhibits
on Waco, Texas, history.

Texas Ranger Hall of Fame and Museum
Box 2570, Waco, Texas 76702-2570
254-750-8631
http://www.texasranger.org/education/index.html
The museum offers guided tours and educational programs
on Texas history, government, criminal investigation
and public safety, geography, and more, including scout
activities, camps, and special programs.

SOURCE NOTES

Chapter 1. To Act or to Wait?

1. David Thibodeau and Leon Whiteson. *A Place Called Waco: A Survivor's Story*. New York: Public Affairs, 1999. Print. 355.

2. "Report to the Deputy Attorney General on the Events at Waco, Texas, February 28 to April 19, 1993." Redacted Version. *US Department of Justice*. 8 Oct. 1993. Web. 27 Aug. 2013. XIII.

3. "Waco: The Inside Story; Chronology of the Siege." *Frontline*. PBS, n.d. Web. 27 Aug. 2013.

4. "Jonestown." *Encyclopedia Britannica*. Encyclopedia Britannica, 2013. Web. 27 Aug. 2013.

5. "Bill of Rights." *The Charters of Freedom*. National Archives, n.d. Web. 27 Aug. 2013.

6. "Report to the Deputy Attorney General on the Events at Waco, Texas, February 28 to April 19, 1993." Redacted Version. *US Department of Justice*. 8 Oct. 1993. Web. 27 Aug. 2013. II.

7. Ibid.

8. Ibid. I.

9. "Waco: The Inside Story; Chronology of the Siege." *Frontline*. PBS, n.d. Web. 27 Aug. 2013.

10. Ibid.

11. Sohra D. Yaqhubi. "Janet Reno, J.D. '63, and Her Long Path from Cambridge to the Capitol." *Harvard Crimson*. Harvard Crimson, 27 May 2013. Web. 27 Aug. 2013.

12. "Report to the Deputy Attorney General on the Events at Waco, Texas, February 28 to April 19, 1993." Redacted Version. *US Department of Justice*. 8 Oct. 1993. Web. 27 Aug. 2013. XI.

Chapter 2. A Short History of the Davidians

1. "Seventh-day Adventist World Church Statistics." *Seventh-day Adventist Church*. General Conference of Seventh-day Adventists, 30 June 2011. Web. 28 Aug. 2013.

2. Dick J. Reavis. *The Ashes of Waco: An Investigation*. New York: Simon, 1995. Print. 55.

3. Ibid. 60.

4. James D. Tabor. *Why Waco?* Berkeley: U of California P, 1995. 58.

5. Dick J. Reavis. *The Ashes of Waco: An Investigation*. New York: Simon, 1995. Print. 75.

6. David B. Kopel and Paul H. Blackman. "The Unwarranted Warrant: The Waco Search Warrant and the Decline of the Fourth Amendment." *Hamline Journal of Public Law and Policy* 18 (Fall 1996). *Constitution.org*. Web. 28 Aug. 2013.

7. Peter J. Boyer, "The Children of Waco." *New Yorker* (May 15, 1995). *PBS: Frontline*. Web. 28 Aug. 2013.

Chapter 3. The Role of the Media

1. David Thibodeau and Leon Whiteson. *A Place Called Waco: A Survivor's Story*. New York: Public Affairs, 1999. Print. 129.

2. Dick J. Reavis. *The Ashes of Waco: An Investigation*. New York: Simon, 1995. Print. 32.

3. Ibid. 39–40.

4. Marc Breault and Martin King. *Inside the Cult*. New York: Signet, 1993. 188.

5. Dick J. Reavis. *The Ashes of Waco: An Investigation*. New York: Simon, 1995. Print. 33.

Chapter 4. A Deadly Confrontation

1. David Thibodeau and Leon Whiteson. *A Place Called Waco: A Survivor's Story*. New York: Public Affairs, 1999. Print. 166.

2. "Waco: The Inside Story; Chronology of the Siege." *Frontline*. PBS, n.d. Web. 27 Aug. 2013.

3. "Report to the Deputy Attorney General on the Events at Waco, Texas, February 28 to April 19, 1993." Redacted Version. *US Department of Justice*. 8 Oct. 1993. Web. 27 Aug. 2013. II.

4. James D. Tabor. "Religious Discourse and Failed Negotiations." *Armageddon in Waco*. Ed. Stuart A. Wright. Chicago: U of Chicago P, 1996. 264.

5. "Report to the Deputy Attorney General on the Events at Waco, Texas, February 28 to April 19, 1993." Redacted Version. *US Department of Justice*. 8 Oct. 1993. Web. 27 Aug. 2013. VIII.

6. Ibid. III.

7. Ibid.

Chapter 5. Talk and Action

1. "Report to the Deputy Attorney General on the Events at Waco, Texas, February 28 to April 19, 1993." Redacted Version. *US Department of Justice*. 8 Oct. 1993. Web. 27 Aug. 2013. II.

2. Ibid. I.

3. Ibid. II.

4. Ibid.

5. James D. Tabor. *Why Waco?* Berkeley: U of California P, 1995. 231n22.

6. Clifford L. Linedecker. *Massacre at Waco, Texas*. New York: St. Martin, 1993. Print. 121.

7. David Thibodeau and Leon Whiteson. *A Place Called Waco: A Survivor's Story*. New York: Public Affairs, 1999. Print. 355–359.

8. "Report to the Deputy Attorney General on the Events at Waco, Texas, February 28 to April 19, 1993." Redacted Version. *US Department of Justice*. 8 Oct. 1993. Web. 27 Aug. 2013. II.

9. "Waco: The Inside Story; Chronology of the Siege." *Frontline*. PBS, n.d. Web. 27 Aug. 2013.

10. "Report to the Deputy Attorney General on the Events at Waco, Texas, February 28 to April 19, 1993." Redacted Version. *US Department of Justice*. 8 Oct. 1993. Web. 27 Aug. 2013. II.

SOURCE NOTES CONTINUED

11. David Thibodeau and Leon Whiteson. *A Place Called Waco: A Survivor's Story.* New York: Public Affairs, 1999. Print. 221.

Chapter 6. Tensions Build

1. "Report to the Deputy Attorney General on the Events at Waco, Texas, February 28 to April 19, 1993." Redacted Version. *US Department of Justice.* 8 Oct. 1993. Web. 27 Aug. 2013. V.

2. Ibid. II.

3. David Thibodeau and Leon Whiteson. *A Place Called Waco: A Survivor's Story.* New York: Public Affairs, 1999. Print. 229.

4. Dick J. Reavis. *The Ashes of Waco: An Investigation.* New York: Simon, 1995. Print. 169.

5. "Report to the Deputy Attorney General on the Events at Waco, Texas, February 28 to April 19, 1993." Redacted Version. *US Department of Justice.* 8 Oct. 1993. Web. 27 Aug. 2013. Appendix C.

6. Dick J. Reavis. *The Ashes of Waco: An Investigation.* New York: Simon, 1995. Print. 211.

7. "Report to the Deputy Attorney General on the Events at Waco, Texas, February 28 to April 19, 1993." Redacted Version. *US Department of Justice.* 8 Oct. 1993. Web. 27 Aug. 2013. II.

8. Ibid.

9. Ibid. III.

10. Ibid.

11. Alex Hannaford. "The Standoff in Waco." *Texas Observer.* Texas Observer, 18 Apr. 2013. Web. 28 Aug. 2013.

Chapter 7. Living Faith or False Religion?

1. "Report to the Deputy Attorney General on the Events at Waco, Texas, February 28 to April 19, 1993." Redacted Version. *US Department of Justice.* 8 Oct. 1993. Web. 27 Aug. 2013. II.

2. Ibid.

3. Dick J. Reavis. *The Ashes of Waco: An Investigation.* New York: Simon, 1995. Print. 251.

4. Hal Crowther. *Gather at the River: Notes from the Post-Millenial South.* Baton Rouge: Louisiana State UP, 2005. 92. *Google Book Search.* Web. 28 Aug. 2013.

5. Dick J. Reavis. *The Ashes of Waco: An Investigation.* New York: Simon, 1995. Print. 103.

6. Ibid. 253.

Chapter 8. Apocalypse Now

1. "Report to the Deputy Attorney General on the Events at Waco, Texas, February 28 to April 19, 1993." Redacted Version. *US Department of Justice.* 8 Oct. 1993. Web. 27 Aug. 2013. XI.

2. James Brovard. *The Destruction of American Liberty*. New York: St. Martin's, 2000. Print. vii.

3. Dick J. Reavis. *The Ashes of Waco: An Investigation*. New York: Simon, 1995. Print. 265.

4. "Report to the Deputy Attorney General on the Events at Waco, Texas, February 28 to April 19, 1993." Redacted Version. *US Department of Justice*. 8 Oct. 1993. Web. 27 Aug. 2013. XII.

5. Ibid.

6. David Thibodeau and Leon Whiteson. *A Place Called Waco: A Survivor's Story*. New York: Public Affairs, 1999. Print. xvii.

7. "Report to the Deputy Attorney General on the Events at Waco, Texas, February 28 to April 19, 1993." Redacted Version. *US Department of Justice*. 8 Oct. 1993. Web. 27 Aug. 2013. XIII.

8. John C. Danforth. "Interim Report to the Deputy Attorney General Concerning the 1993 Confrontation at the Mt. Carmel Complex, Waco, Texas." *Office of Special Council John C. Danforth*, 21 July 2000. 20. *Carol Moore's Waco Pages*. Web. 28 Aug. 2013.

Chapter 9. The Aftermath

1. David Thibodeau and Leon Whiteson. *A Place Called Waco: A Survivor's Story*. New York: Public Affairs, 1999. Print. 355.

2. "Report to the Deputy Attorney General on the Events at Waco, Texas, February 28 to April 19, 1993." Redacted Version. *US Department of Justice*. 8 Oct. 1993. Web. 27 Aug. 2013. XIV.

3. "Oklahoma City Bombing." *Encyclopedia Britannica*. Encyclopedia Britannica, 2013. Web. 28 Aug. 2013.

4. John C. Danforth. "Interim Report to the Deputy Attorney General Concerning the 1993 Confrontation at the Mt. Carmel Complex, Waco, Texas." *Office of Special Council John C. Danforth*, 21 July 2000. i. *Carol Moore's Waco Pages*. Web. 28 Aug. 2013.

5. "John C. Danforth Biography." *Bryan Cave*. Bryan Cave International Consulting, n.d. Web. 28 Aug. 2013.

6. "Child Survivors Recall Waco Fire 10 Years On." *ABCNews*. ABCNews, n.d. Web. 28 Aug. 2013.

7. Connie Farrow. "US Government 'Did No Evil' in Waco Tragedy but Lacked Honesty." *The Independent*. The Independent, 22 July 2000. Web. 28 Aug. 2013.

8. David Thibodeau and Leon Whiteson. *A Place Called Waco: A Survivor's Story*. New York: Public Affairs, 1999. Print. 349.

9. Jayne Seminare Docherty. *Learning Lessons from Waco: When the Parties Bring Their Gods to the Negotiation Table*. Syracuse, NY: Syracuse UP, 2001. 277–288. Print.

10. Marc Breault and Martin King. *Inside the Cult*. New York: Signet, 1993. Print. 342.

INDEX

ABOUT THE AUTHOR

Scott Gillam is a former English teacher and an editor of social studies and language arts textbooks. He is the author of *Civil Liberties* in the ABDO Essential Viewpoints series and biographies of Andrew Carnegie, Steve Jobs, Rachel Carson, and Sigmund Freud in the Essential Lives series.

ABOUT THE CONSULTANT

Eugene V. Gallagher is the Rosemary Park Professor of Religious Studies at Connecticut College. He is the coauthor of *Why Waco? Cults and the Battle for Religious Freedom in America* and numerous essays on the Branch Davidians, among other topics. He is also the author of *The New Religious Movements Experience in America* and coeditor of the five volume *Introduction to New and Alternative Religions in the United States*.